D0481916

LIFE'S A BARK

WHAT DOGS TEACH US ABOUT LIFE AND LOVE

larry kay

 sourcebooks

This publication is designed to provide accurate and authoritative information in
regard to the subject matter covered. It is sold with the understanding that the publisher is not engaged in rendering legal, accounting, or other professional service. If legal
advice or other expert assistance is required, the services of a competent professional
person should be sought. —*From a Declaration of Principles Jointly Adopted by a Committee of the American Bar Association and a Committee of Publishers and Associations*

Published by Sourcebooks, Inc.
P.O. Box 4410, Naperville, Illinois 60567-4410
(630) 961-3900
Fax: (630) 961-2168
www.sourcebooks.com

Library of Congress Cataloging-in-Publication data is on file with the publisher.

Printed and bound in the United States of America.
WOZ 10 9 8 7 6 5 4 3 2 1

★ DEDICATION ★

For Leslie, Mike, Paul, and all who
make lives better for (and with) dogs.

INTRODUCTION

What's in a bark? Of course dogs bark to get attention or to protect themselves or their owners. But our canine friends vocalize much more than that. We actually live in a world of happy barks, sad barks, barks of fear, anger, anxiety, pain, excitement, glee, gratitude, pride, belonging. Dogs also teach us the qualities of quiet. The absence of a bark, howl, or growl often means contentment, alertness, guilt, wonder, respect.

There's a lot we can learn about life and love from our canine friends. In fact, the latest research indicates that dog EQ (emotional intelligence quotient) is equal to, if not higher than, human EQ. Dogs show high levels of empathy, compassion, care, trust, and distrust. When it comes to emotions and personality, it may well be the dog, not the chimpanzee, that is our closest kin. And more and more, we humans are treating dogs that way.

Treat me like a dog...please. Maybe it sounds funny, but the days when being "treated like a dog" was a bad thing are *long* gone. Today, dogs are living the good life! Advances in nutrition and care have dramatically improved dogs' lifespans. Training focuses on positive reinforcement and helps dogs develop their delightful personalities along with good manners. That's why elite handlers of show dogs and movie dogs now emphasize positive, reward-based methods. With all of this and other canine-friendly developments (even such things as doggie yoga and dog play gyms), it's a great time to be a loved dog in a forever home.

Like our canine friends, we humans also thrive when we're treated with praise, respect, encouragement, and love. What if we treat everyone—ourselves included—the way we pamper our pooches? What if we apply the canine approach to life and its deep emotional intelligence to our human relationships? How might we change for the better by taking lessons from the dog's playbook of life? That's exactly what this book—and the dogs in it—set out to teach us.

Let's woof wisely. Let's live magnificent, vibrant lives. Let's help our world bark a little happier. It's actually easy. Much of it is in our nature, especially when we tap into that power of positivity. If dogs can do it, so can we...when we get out of our own way.

 ## TRY THIS:

Praise yourself. Seriously. Right now. Even if it makes you feel self-conscious, give yourself a compliment. Treat yourself positively. Treat yourself like a loved dog.

As you grant yourself the positive attention you deserve, you'll set yourself up to be happier for life. It's like learning to ride a bike or play a new game. Dogs play games passionately. So can we. Let's make a game of treating ourselves well and we'll all benefit.

Since life's a bark, let's make a joyful noise!

Larry Kay
www.facebook.com/positivelywoof
www.positivelywoof.com

THINK BIG.

Spirited dogs teach us the meaning of living large and thinking optimistically. Whether they're chasing squirrels, dragging the biggest stick they can find, or greeting you like royalty, dogs share their excitement effortlessly and usually do it on a grand scale.

We humans often box ourselves up, worrying about others' opinions of our decisions or actions or automatically adopting a pessimistic view in the face of a challenge. On the other hand (or paw), being around optimism can change our mood and possibilities. What if you treated yourself and others with dog-like optimism? Failure might not matter anymore!

TRY THIS:

Drag a big stick in a park while thinking about something that's important to you. When people give you funny looks, dare to be thought of as nutty, or even wild.

SMILE AND THE WHOLE WORLD SMILES WITH YOU.

Dogs smile naturally. Maybe that's why they easily bring us so much joy.

Smiling makes us look more attractive and has health benefits too: lower blood pressure, strengthened immune system, and released endorphins (for pain relief) and serotonin (for sleep). When we receive a smile, our mood is brightened.

TRY THIS:

Smile in public for no reason. Smile at someone else who is smiling too.

5

BORN TO BE WILD.

Sure, most dogs like being walked on a leash. But let's face it, they also really *love* to go off-leash, sprinting and exploring without direction or plan.

We too have a need for unbridled freedom, even though we have become accustomed to our own "leashes" of safety, security, and belonging. So how do we keep that untamed spark alive while still feeling safe and secure?

TRY THIS:

Dance naked around your home. You'll be free from limitations and any prying eyes.

TRY THIS:

Run barefoot through a field.

When dogs run, their paws
paint the earth with grace.

"BEST FRIEND" IS MY MIDDLE NAME.

Dogs bond naturally with humans, with a loyalty and empathy like no other animal. Some say we have co-evolved since our days together as cave dwellers.

When times are tough, how do you give a helping hand and a patient ear to others? Do you encourage and celebrate victories great and small, or do you beat yourself up for something that went imperfectly?

Ask yourself: Are you being a true friend to yourself? If not, it's hard to be a good one to others.

TRY THIS:

List what you like best about yourself as a friend. For one day, practice one of your favorite qualities. The next day, practice another.

I ALWAYS MISS YOU.

Even though we try to reassure them when we leave that everything will be okay, many dogs have anxiety when they are left alone. They show distress by making a lot of noise, destroying stuff, or trying to escape.

We humans are social animals just like dogs. We miss loved ones, friends, and even inanimate things and places. But can we figure out how to embrace our moments of solitude even when we feel the pain of loneliness?

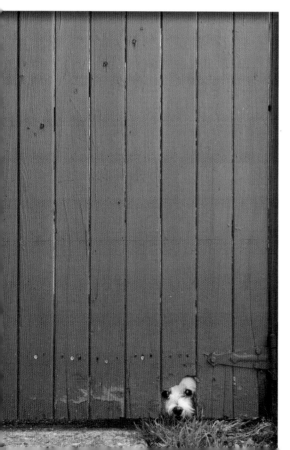

TRY THIS:

The next time you feel lonely, allow yourself five minutes to howl. Then do something nice for yourself.

HONOR MY FEELINGS.

Yes, dogs experience the same basic emotions that we do: joy, love, sadness, fear, anger, shame. When dogs are fearful, they fight, flee, or freeze.

Humans have the same fight, flight, or freeze reaction when it comes to negative emotions, but unlike dogs, we can struggle to show or let ourselves feel positive emotions too. Yet when we acknowledge our feelings, we start to feel better. Honoring our emotions also paves the way for stronger relationships and greater happiness overall.

TRY THIS:

Allow yourself to feel each of these basic emotions: joy, love, sadness, fear, anger, shame. Which emotions feel safe, familiar? When you feel fear, do you want to fight, flee, or freeze? Which emotions make you want to "numb out"?

I'M BEAUTIFUL AND SO ARE YOU.

Dogs can see the supermodel in us. Can we see it in them—and in ourselves?

Beauty is being comfortable in our own skin, regardless of what we look like. Self-love and self-acceptance are keys to unlocking the door to true beauty.

TRY THIS:

While you're in the shower, say "you're beautiful" as you scrub every part of yourself.

DON'T JUDGE ME.

When dogs trust someone, they seem to open their hearts fully, accepting without judgment.

What's at risk if we do the same, letting go of our judgments or at least not allowing ourselves to be ruled by them? How is our judgment of someone also a look into our own mirror?

Is the occasional claw on the nose or embarrassment worth it with this friend? There are numerous rewards for us when we accept others as they are, so let's look to dogs for inspiration, starting with gratitude and simple goodness.

TRY THIS:

The next time a friend or loved one admits something embarrassing to you, give him or her a hug and say, "I love you no matter what."

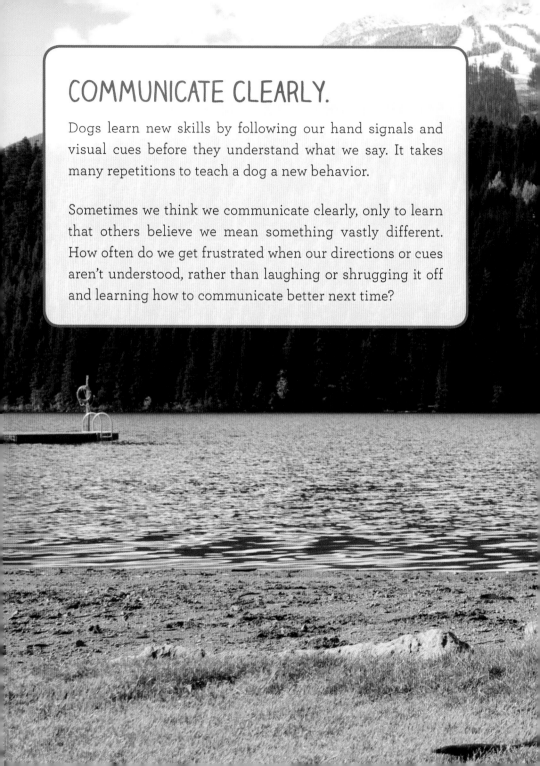

COMMUNICATE CLEARLY.

Dogs learn new skills by following our hand signals and visual cues before they understand what we say. It takes many repetitions to teach a dog a new behavior.

Sometimes we think we communicate clearly, only to learn that others believe we mean something vastly different. How often do we get frustrated when our directions or cues aren't understood, rather than laughing or shrugging it off and learning how to communicate better next time?

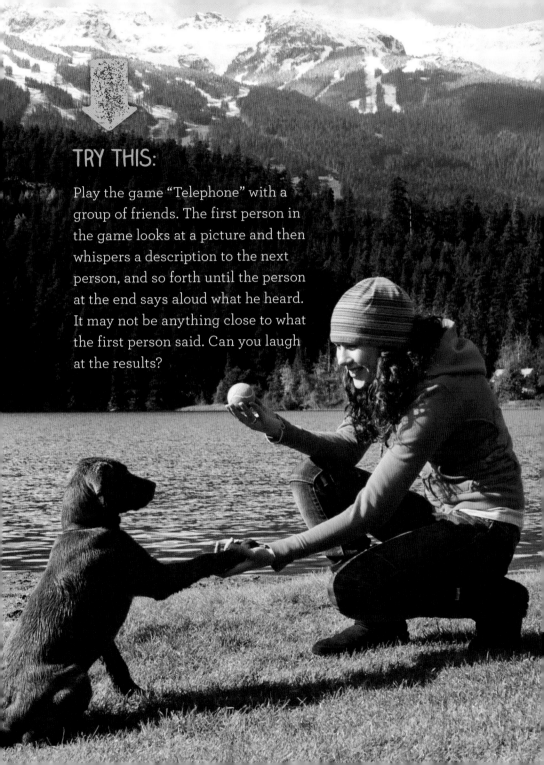

TRY THIS:

Play the game "Telephone" with a group of friends. The first person in the game looks at a picture and then whispers a description to the next person, and so forth until the person at the end says aloud what he heard. It may not be anything close to what the first person said. Can you laugh at the results?

LISTEN WELL.

A dog may not understand the subtleties of what we say, nor can he speak in words. But when we need to talk, a loyal dog stays by us with patient attention.

Sometimes our chatter and problem-solving get in the way of simply listening. Good listening means being curious and patient. Listen well by using the L-O-V-E system: Listen, Observe, Verify, and Empathize.

TRY THIS:

Listen to someone without giving any advice. Pretend you're a dog who has no words and no place to go, but who is simply a master of patience, curiosity, and L-O-V-E.

FOLLOW THE RIGHT LEADER.

The myth about dog pack psychology is that dogs need a bully boss. However, research shows that dogs prefer to follow leaders who provide safety, security, well-being, and play.

It's important to look at how we respond to leaders too. Do we put them up on pedestals, only to throw them under the bus when they inevitably make a mistake? Do we resist or rebel against leadership or follow unquestioningly? Do we dare to try being leaders ourselves?

TRY THIS:

Imagine the leaders you know as dogs. What kind of dogs are they? What are "their" dog packs like?

KEEP ME SAFE AND SECURE.

Dogs, like humans, are hard-wired to avoid pain and situations that seem unsafe. Dog packs provide safety in numbers. A good forever home provides the safety and security they crave too.

Safety means different things to different people. Some people are seemingly carefree (or even careless) about safety, while others' needs for safety are ever-present.

 ## TRY THIS:

Close your eyes and think of what makes you feel safe. What does *safety* feel like for you? What do you do when you feel safe? Can you bring up that feeling when you feel *un*safe?

MAKE MY HOME A "FOREVER HOME."

Every dog deserves a forever home, which means a lifetime in one home filled with love, affection, and the basic necessities that help life thrive. But each year, millions of dogs never get to experience this, either drifting between homes, spending their whole lives in animal shelters waiting for one, or on the streets.

Every person also deserves a home. Yet homelessness challenges our society and sometimes impacts our own lives. If we have a home, do we sometimes take it for granted?

TRY THIS:

Close your eyes. Imagine yourself homeless. Open your eyes. Be grateful for three things in your home. Without guilt or shame, consider one thing that would make your home better. Now imagine yourself volunteering to provide homes for others.

I'M A PROTECTOR.

Most dogs are gentle by nature, but they're also fierce protectors of what they love. Sometimes it's helpful. Other times it's not necessary.

Are we willing to protect the people and things we value and love? What do we protect that doesn't need protecting? What fear keeps us from protecting what is most important to us?

TRY THIS:

Imagine you're a dog. Protect an object that represents something important. Growl, bark, bare your teeth to protect it. Feel your power, even as you quiet down.

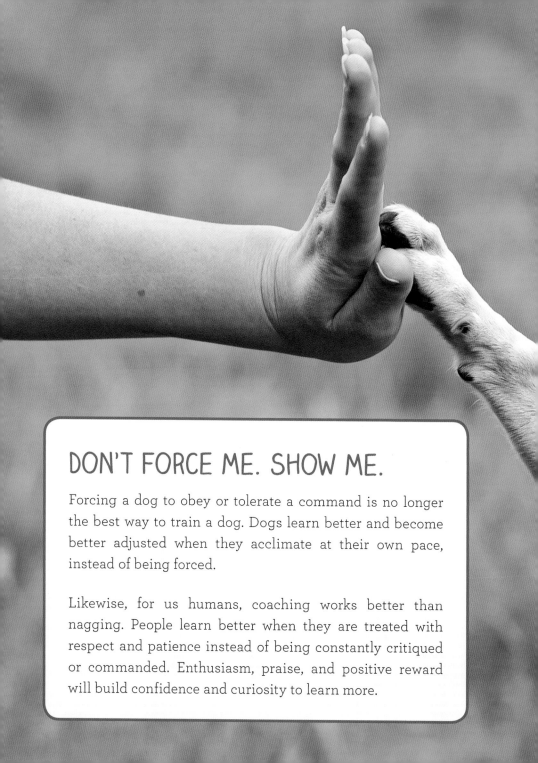

DON'T FORCE ME. SHOW ME.

Forcing a dog to obey or tolerate a command is no longer the best way to train a dog. Dogs learn better and become better adjusted when they acclimate at their own pace, instead of being forced.

Likewise, for us humans, coaching works better than nagging. People learn better when they are treated with respect and patience instead of being constantly critiqued or commanded. Enthusiasm, praise, and positive reward will build confidence and curiosity to learn more.

TRY THIS:

The next time you instruct someone, use extra encouragement and praise, realizing that it will not be done perfectly. Bonus points if you provide a reward.

PRAISE ME.

Dogs love praise. Positive dog training emphasizes praise as the most basic reward. It's more important than treats. Our well-timed praise teaches good manners, increases joy, and allows a dog's personality to flourish.

Praising is a skill: the more we give and receive it, the better we become at it. It's a good idea to evaluate from time to time how we give praise in our lives and how we receive it. Are we generous or stingy with it? Do we believe that praise will add or subtract motivation? Is it easier for you to give or to receive praise?

TRY THIS:

Look at yourself in the mirror and praise yourself daily for a week. At the end of the week, is praise easier to give and receive? Now try daily praise with a friend or loved one for a week. How does that feel at the end of the week?

WHETHER OR NOT YOU TEACH ME, I ALWAYS LEARN.

A dog constantly tries to figure out what will earn rewards, even if that means doing things that we don't want her to do. Until we set the rules or direct a dog's behavior, she will "learn" on her own.

How do we figure out our world? Do we seek permission or ask for forgiveness if our risk-taking has negative consequences? How do we hold ourselves back from taking risks?

TRY THIS:

Give yourself permission to do something good for yourself.

PRACTICE IMPULSE CONTROL.

We ask our dogs to practice impulse control, such as sitting still for praise or a treat reward. With patient practice, they eventually learn each behavior without needing to be rewarded anymore.

When we practice impulse control, we thrive too. As we build our own good habits, let's treat ourselves with kind patience and a little humor too, rewarding our efforts and forgiving our mistakes.

TRY THIS:

Think of an impulse you would benefit from controlling. Then think about all the benefits of your success. Practice that impulse control three times and reward yourself in a healthy way for each success.

DISCIPLINE ME...IN A NICE WAY, PLEASE!

Disciplining a dog doesn't need to be harsh. When positive motivation fails, the dog trainer needs to redirect the dog's attention to something the dog will likely succeed at and return to the original lesson later.

We need far less discipline to do something when we're enthusiastic about it or when it's already an established habit. But in most other cases, discipline is vital to motivate us. The question is: Do we discipline ourselves by beating ourselves up, or do we find constructive ways to encourage us forward?

TRY THIS:

When you have a task that you're not enthusiastic about, break it down into small parts. Praise yourself for each part completed.

I RESPECT YOU.

Dogs naturally respect humans who take care of them. They express respect for those same things over and over and over.

What is it like to respect ourselves (and others) the way dogs respect us? Can we show that respect repeatedly?

TRY THIS:

Pretend you're a dog. Look at yourself in the mirror, smile like a dog, and say three things you respect yourself for. Say the same three things again until you begin to believe them.

LOVE ME AS I AM.

Dogs accept themselves as they are. They easily show affection for us as we are and don't hesitate to "ask" for our affection in return. They seem naturally able to get over upsets, mistakes, guilt, and shame quickly.

When we treat ourselves and each other like this, we show easy acceptance, affection, forgiveness, respect, and a smile. And trust me, that goes a long way in the human and canine worlds.

TRY THIS:

When you have a negative thought, interrupt that pessimistic pattern by acting like a dog: smile and pant. Bonus points for scratching your head with your foot.

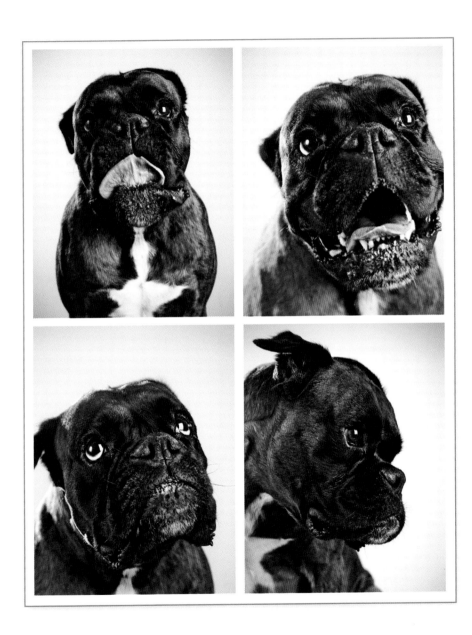

YOU'RE EASY TO LOVE.

Do dogs really love unconditionally? While we humans sit and debate whether that's true, dogs are content to accept us as we are.

Acceptance and self-assurance are at the core of a dog's love. So is loyalty. Sweetness. Patience. Protection. Playfulness. Respect. Adoration. And don't forget slobbery kisses.

TRY THIS:

Kiss yourself and say, "I love you and accept you as you are."

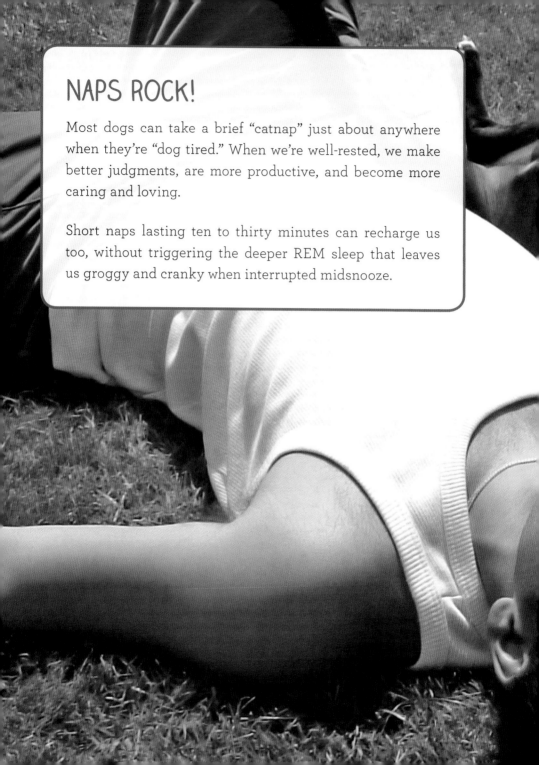

NAPS ROCK!

Most dogs can take a brief "catnap" just about anywhere when they're "dog tired." When we're well-rested, we make better judgments, are more productive, and become more caring and loving.

Short naps lasting ten to thirty minutes can recharge us too, without triggering the deeper REM sleep that leaves us groggy and cranky when interrupted midsnooze.

TRY THIS:

Take a nap during your lunch break. If that's not feasible, try falling asleep while watching Animal Planet.

THE BLESSING OF A GOOD BELLY RUB.

Unless a dog has been traumatized in the past, a good belly rub is a cherished form of touch. Canines' vulnerable "belly to the sky" position shows how much they trust us to treat them well.

Unless *we* have been traumatized, hugging and touching will also relieve our stress, improve trust, and increase bonding with others. So it's a good thing to practice.

TRY THIS:

Next time you're with a loved one, give a spontaneous hug, kiss, or friendly squeeze (whatever's appropriate). Bonus points if they return the gesture.

SHOW OFF!

Dogs thrive on being noticed, so they'd rather show off and get attention for bad behavior than get no attention at all.

But showing off doesn't automatically make us (or others) egomaniacs. In fact, it can build self-esteem, as long as we don't base our self-worth on others' reactions. Take time to celebrate the positive show-off in others and in yourself.

TRY THIS:

The next time you go grocery shopping, enter the store in a grand style as if you're going onstage in front of a full audience of adoring fans. Bonus points if someone sees you doing it.

LET'S DISCOVER NEW TRICKS TOGETHER.

When we train our dogs clearly and consistently, with patience and play, we also strengthen our bond with them. If we watch closely, we'll discover tricks our dogs offer without being asked...and we may even discover new things about ourselves.

These newly discovered tricks are like shared experiences that become life's great memories. In relationships (whether human or canine), we can even develop a shorthand for them, where one word or signal communicates a specific shared experience.

TRY THIS:

Create an elaborate handshake with a friend or loved one. Bonus points if it becomes your regular greeting.

A little help can
make life great again.

TRY THIS:

Give a little help to a friend.
Ask for a little help. Which
is easier for you?

I HAVE MY OWN STYLE.

Dogs have a vast range of personalities across and within every breed. There are more than 175 official and more than 350 unofficial dog breeds in the U.S., plus countless mystery mutts. That's a whole lotta personality.

But we humans often limit our own style and sense of self because of what we look like, what we were born into, or what others tell us we are. With all these confines, how do we even begin to define who we are, let alone show it?

TRY THIS:

Walk like you're the biggest and most beautiful dog in town: a brand-new hound of unknown origin. You don't need to do anything to be given respect.

GREATNESS IS EASY.

A dog easily sees greatness in a loving companion who consistently provides basic food, shelter, and safety. This consistent gratitude begets the ease in greatness.

How do we recognize greatness in others and in ourselves? It's important to ask ourselves whether we can see greatness as easily as we see flaws. What would life be like if you let your own greatness shine the way a dog might see it?

TRY THIS:

For one minute, pretend all that you are and everything that you have has been given to you. Pause and revel in your gratitude for the greatness of these gifts.

UNLEASH MY AWESOMENESS.

It's easy for us to tell dogs that they're good, handsome, pretty, funny, smart, and awesome. Dogs don't deny our compliments or downplay them by replying, "Aww, shucks, it's nothing."

How often do we deny our awesomeness? Do we hope others will notice us, just so we can pretend it doesn't matter? Why are we uncomfortable about receiving a compliment?

 TRY THIS:

Look at yourself in the mirror. Pretend that your reflection is an awesome dog. Say your name enthusiastically and compliment yourself for ten seconds. Expert trick: do it for a minute.

GREET YOUR NEIGHBOR.

Most dogs need to be taught "good manners" with neighbor dogs and people: no biting or unwanted behavior. Good greetings are typically brief. A well-socialized dog can add delight to a whole neighborhood.

We humans haven't had formal training on how to be good neighbors, per se. So all we can do is hope our "good manners" are sufficient. But what would our communities be like if we learned how to be **great** neighbors?

TRY THIS:

Next time you see a neighbor, pause to give a friendly, brief greeting. Then move on without expectation, unless the neighbor reciprocates with a longer greeting.

LET'S PLAY ALREADY!

Dogs are hard-wired to play. Their "bowing" position (like in the picture below) is their invitation to play and is nearly universal among dog breeds throughout the world.

Play relieves stress, builds social health, and releases endorphins (for pain relief) and serotonin (for sleep). It's also important to play fairly. After all, playing is more than a competition with winners and losers.

TRY THIS:

Schedule playtime for yourself or with a friend. Don't let anything bump it from your schedule...except for maybe another spontaneous invitation to play.

Play well with others.
Share.

Go all out with a friend.

I'M BIGGER THAN I LOOK.

In a dog pack, it's not uncommon for a little dog to act like the boss. Many herding dogs are small in size but fearless in ordering big, hulking cattle around...and sometimes ordering people too.

Is bigger always bossier or better? Often, no. So why do we sometimes surround ourselves with big things or try to make ourselves look bigger?

TRY THIS:

Imagine that every vehicle on the road is a dog. What breed might yours be? Pretend you're a big truck and then a small used car. Practice being happy and confident in both. Drive carefully while doing this.

I DON'T HAVE TO LIKE EVERYONE, AND NOT EVERYONE LIKES ME.

Dogs tend to tolerate our idiosyncrasies and seemingly arbitrary behavior far better than we tolerate theirs.

Not liking someone or not being liked by someone doesn't mean that we need to be disrespectful or unkind to them, but rather that our tastes and desires just don't mesh with theirs. Understanding and respecting our differences is a big part of having authentic, honest, and ultimately happier interactions.

TRY THIS:

Laugh at an idiosyncrasy of yours. Bonus points for having a friend or loved one laugh with you.

LET'S GO ON AN ADVENTURE.

When dogs explore a new place, they dive in nosefirst. Excitement and curiosity usually overcome any fear.

Adventure is important for our spirit, body, mind, and emotional well-being. It feeds our resilience and happiness to get out in the fresh air, exercise, and try new challenges and experiences.

TRY THIS:

Go to a familiar place. Find at least one thing about it that you never noticed before and marvel at that. Bring that curiosity to your next real adventure.

WALKIES DAILY, PLEASE.

On the whole, dog owners walk more than people who don't own dogs. For most dogs, walks are the highlight of the day.

Regular walks can reduce stress, help sleep, improve your sex life, reduce sugar addiction, prevent sickness, and heal disease. Plus, walking is fun.

TRY THIS:

Take a familiar walk. Observe something new. Delight in the smell of something, even if it's just the crisp, fresh air.

SHOW ME THE HAPPY.

Many dogs seem to have endless joy and optimism. They're also naturally brilliant at showing their excitement and happiness, even with a simple tail wag.

The more we practice "showing the happy," the better we get at it—and the better we'll feel. Even forcing ourselves into a little happiness can change our whole mind-set and bring happiness to ourselves and others.

TRY THIS:

The next time you feel sad or cranky, don't fight it. Be grumpy for five minutes. Then pretend to be happy for one full minute. Then choose to be grumpy or happy for the next three minutes. Repeat as necessary and you'll be smiling genuinely before you know it.

When you're happy,

    put your whole body into it.

AN INSTANT ATTITUDE ADJUSTMENT.

A dog's greeting can wipe away the emotional grime of a bad day. Whether we hit a home run or struck out, got a raise or got fired, a loved dog treats us like a rock star, no matter what.

How do we let our inner rock star shine, even on days that produced only sour music? Without denying a struggle or setback, can we stay open to the goodness and blessings in our lives?

TRY THIS:

The next time you have a setback, pretend for one minute that you're a dog. Wag your tail, run in circles, hop, bark, smile, pant. It will take the edge off for a moment and may change your state of mind for the whole day.

REWARD MY EFFORT.

When dogs are rewarded for trying new behaviors, they blossom with confidence, self-esteem, and joy.

We humans are also more motivated to learn and become more skilled when we are praised for trying. When we're encouraged, we are more apt to think outside the box: experiment, create, discover. So how can we better praise ourselves for trying?

TRY THIS:

Play the dog training game called "The 101 Box." Do ten different things with an empty box. Praise yourself for each new thing. Next time, try another ten. See if you can do up to 101 different things with the box.

BE QUICK TO FORGIVE.

As long as dogs trust us, they forgive our mistakes easily. They look with optimism for the best in us. But when dogs don't trust us, they're always on guard.

When is it easier to forgive another's mistakes? When we are able to feel grateful and remember the abundance in life, it is easier to forgive mistakes. Does forgiveness seem like we're being pushovers? Can we forgive and also have healthy boundaries?

TRY THIS:

Forgive yourself. And then you can forgive others. You'll feel better for it, guaranteed.

FORGIVE MY TRESPASSES.

There is no such thing as a perfect dog or a perfect dog trainer. Mistakes happen. But dogs always forgive their teachers and themselves.

If we don't make mistakes, we're not stretching our abilities. We can challenge ourselves to forgive mistakes as easily as our canine friends do. Which is easier for you—to forgive others' mistakes or to forgive your own? When we don't forgive, what are the possible consequences to ourselves and others?

TRY THIS:

Set a goal to make ten mistakes a day. Reward yourself for making all ten.

TEACH ME HEALTHY BOUNDARIES.

Dogs don't like being told "no" any more than we do. But reasonable, clear boundaries keep them safe and keep possessions from being destroyed. Rewarding a dog for obeying boundaries will build good habits.

When we set reasonable boundaries in a healthy, clear way, we show others what we feel is safe and respectful for us. When we teach ourselves boundaries, we become better at self-discipline.

TRY THIS:

Set up a circle of chairs around you. Name each chair as a boundary in your life. Remove one chair and declare what boundary you are choosing to remove. Honor that, as well as those you are keeping.

TOYS DON'T LAST FOREVER.

Some dogs like to shred toys, while others like to carry a toy until it's no longer special. Dogs prefer short play periods with a toy.

Over time, unused toys become clutter for us too, getting in the way of things that are far more valuable to us right now. What old possession once had special meaning for you but no longer holds any usefulness to you? Have you said, "I'll use it again...someday," but never do?

TRY THIS:

Give away something that used to be valuable, but now feels dusty or worthless. Imagine a new person enjoying it. If necessary, use it one last time before you give it away.

CHALLENGE ME.

Dogs that are destructive tend to have nothing better to do. They're often smart but bored and need to be challenged... and rewarded.

New challenges can also propel us into greater success and even whole new ways of being. But we often shy away from viewing challenges as fun. Does our fear (of failure, success, or change) block us from trying?

TRY THIS:

Write one new goal onto ten pieces of paper, crumple them up, and toss each into a basket about three feet away. Envision each toss as throwing away one part of what's blocking you from completing your goal. Create a reward for yourself just for playing this game.

I LOVE AND LIVE TO SERVE.

Dogs serve naturally. They love to follow good leaders. As leaders, they live to serve their pack.

When we serve, we make our world better, which makes us better too. When we give, we also receive.

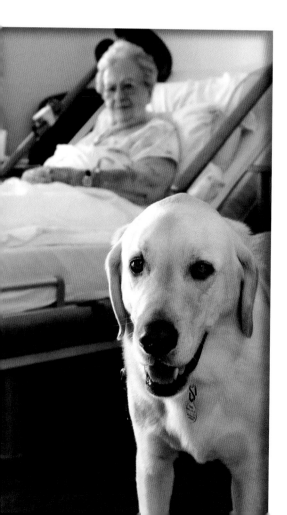

TRY THIS:

Volunteer in your community. Know that your contribution makes a difference and adds love. How do you feel during and after each act? Any unexpected consequences?

EMBRACE HUMILITY.

Dogs became "man's best friend" by delighting in following our good leadership. They were domesticated, in part, because their nature is suited to be our humble sidekicks.

That wonderful sense of humility is also inside every genuine "thank you." The humble act means that we delight in serving, listening, or caring for another's well-being without needing to be in the spotlight ourselves.

TRY THIS:

Do a simple act of service for a friend or loved one without being asked and without expecting anything in return. If you're asked why you're doing this, say something like, "Because you're awesome and you deserve it."

OLD DOGS *CAN* LEARN NEW TRICKS.

Actually, old dogs can be calmer and more focused than young dogs, which often makes learning easier, especially when praise and rewards are offered.

We too can learn new tricks. There are countless examples of people who start something new at retirement and then excel at it. All it takes is a little patience and perseverance.

TRY THIS:

Choose something you've wanted to learn or improve. Assume that you've already done it. Then evaluate how you accomplished it. Now you can start taking steps toward achieving your new trick.

KEEP ME HEALTHY.

On the average, dogs live longer nowadays due to advances in nutrition, medicine, and general care that good humans provide. But sometimes we provide too much. For example, overfeeding may harm a dog's health even though it seems like a caring act of love.

Sometimes we value immediate gratification over long-term benefits to our well-being. How do we balance discipline and desire to instantly please not only our dogs, but also ourselves?

TRY THIS:

The next time you have an impulse to do something unhealthy, instead tell yourself, "Good human. I love you," every five minutes for the following half hour. Then make a choice on whether to act on that impulse.

SOME THINGS ARE GOOD FOR ME, EVEN THOUGH I DON'T LIKE THEM.

Why do dogs love to romp in the water but hate baths?

Even when we have enthusiasm and a vivid vision of how to achieve a goal, we sometimes need to use every ounce of discipline just to get motivated to work toward it. Yet when the "torture" is over, we almost always enjoy the results…even when we won't admit it out loud.

TRY THIS:

Do something that you've been putting off. Or even just a small part of it. Reward yourself with a treat and a pat on the head.

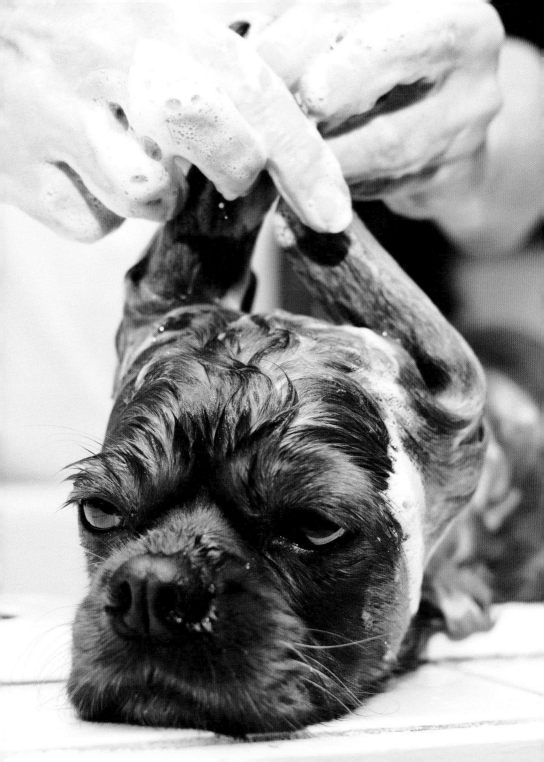

Rejoice in nature.

Let the outside world
embrace and enthrall you.

JOY OH JOY OH JOY, OH JOY!

Dogs are naturals at expressing all kinds of joy. They don't hold back. They are simply genuine with joy. We can be too, if we give ourselves the courage to do so.

TRY THIS:

By yourself, put some music on and dance for joy. Pretend you're a dog and you're moving for the sheer fun of it. Bonus points for any moves you pull off that you'd be embarrassed to do in front of others.

LIVE IN THE MOMENT.

Dogs live in the moment so naturally that we sometimes wonder whether they have a memory at all.

Wake up grateful. Add a smile early. Focus on what you're doing right now even when other tasks await. Bring joy, kindness, and respect to others...and to yourself.

TRY THIS:

Do a random act of kindness for yourself or others today. Take a moment to breathe in the joy you feel afterward.

LIFE AFTER DOG.

Dogs teach us about loss. To have a dog is to sign up for the inevitable sadness that we will probably outlive our companion, our friend, that sometimes-knuckleheaded beast who perhaps accepted us more than we accepted ourselves.

To deny the pain is to deny that we live, that we love, that we matter to each other. And our canine companions would never want that.

TRY THIS:

If you are grieving a loss (human, canine, or otherwise), honor your feelings. What you feel keeps your loved ones alive in your heart, connecting you with them always.

TREAT ME LIKE A DOG...REALLY!

Today, we sometimes treat dogs better than we treat people...and ourselves. Dogs make it fun to treat them well.

But that doesn't mean we can't give ourselves the same royal treatment we give our pooches. It's important to think about what we are naturally good at when it comes to treating others well (like our dogs) and then follow through with that behavior in each aspect of our lives. How do we make it easy for others to treat us well? Do we get in our own way?

TRY THIS:

Do at least one thing to pamper yourself today. Bonus points if you can keep up the habit for a week.

Life's a bark.
Make a joyful noise!

★ ACKNOWLEDGMENTS ★

This book might have been homeless without the positive reinforcement of my dear friend and agent, Paula Munier of Talcott Notch. Paula shaped this project like a master trick trainer.

Thank you to Sourcebooks Senior Editor Stephanie Bowen for giving this book the most loving forever home. Stephanie shepherded this book's words and pictures like the ultimate Border collie. Gratitude to the photographers who captured these moments like champion sight hounds. Please contact me via Facebook so I can honor your work directly.

In my creative studio, daily thanks to my assistants Nora Frankovich and Allison Walls, who loyally leap through the agility course of development and logistics on all my pet projects with terrier tenacity.

Thank you to my scribe tribe, especially animal philosopher Dr. Gary Steiner, Steven Goldman, George Joyce, Les Sinclair, Dr. Darryl Tippens, Elaine Zicree, and Marc Scott Zicree. Big barks to my Facebook fans and BlogPaws colleagues whose love of dogs inspires me daily.

To all generations of my loving family: thanks for the lifelong "belly rub." Blessings to the men of the ManKind Project's Valley Oaks I-Group for accepting both my gold and my shadows.

I was dogless while writing and photo editing this book, which gave poignancy to the creative process. Wags to my dog training clients and colleagues, neighbors and friends who gave me bonus time with their loved dogs, cats, and assorted critters. You gave my woofs your wisdom.

I hope we can all embark on many more adventures together!

Best barks, **Larry**

The End.

★ ABOUT THE AUTHOR ★

Larry Kay believes that when we discover pets, we discover ourselves. He coauthored the award-winning *Training the Best Dog Ever* with Bo Obama's dog trainer, the late Dawn Sylvia-Stasiewicz. He also created and produced *Animal Wow,* which has become the most award-winning dog care and safety DVD for kids.

His canine journalism credits include columnist and contributing editor for *Dog Fancy* magazine and reporting on the Westminster Dog Show for AOL. Larry's pet projects include editorial relationships in animal welfare (endorsed by the American Humane Association) and veterinarians (American Animal Hospital Association).

As a motivational speaker, Larry talks to audiences and mentors individuals with wisdom from *Life's a Bark,* inspiring people to pursue their life's missions and achieve peak performance. When his schedule permits, he also helps people train their dogs, always using reward-based, positive training.

Larry celebrates our human–animal bond by creating and producing world-class media projects, including a forthcoming dog-themed reality TV series. He has produced and written for Disney, *The Muppets,* and PBS.

Larry's popular Facebook page shares daily inspiration, news, and entertainment with dog-loving fans. He invites you to share your canine life, love, and photos.

visit Larry online

www.facebook.com/positivelywoof

www.positivelywoof.com

celebrate our bond

Photo Credits